Kate Middleton | Passage

New Poems

GIRAMONDO POETS

Kate Middleton | Passage

First published 2017
from the Writing & Society Research Centre
at the University of Western Sydney
by the Giramondo Publishing Company
PO Box 752 Artarmon NSW 1570 Australia
www.giramondopublishing.com

Designed by Harry Williamson
Typeset by Andrew Davies
in 10/16.5 pt Baskerville BT

Printed and bound by Ligare
Distributed in Australia by NewSouth Books

National Library of Australia
Cataloguing-in-Publication data:

Middleton, Kate, author
Title: Passages
Kate Middleton

ISBN 978-1-925336-43-6 (pbk)

For my parents Kay and Graham

Contents

Lyric

after Dan Beachy-Quick

The whale by the whale's own light
The song by song's own mesh of I
of we: the zoomorph of lion, man
and gentle coo of lullaby

Voice—I, we—dissects this sea
and whale carves history from the bone
lions pace the den of sleep
and explorer's ship moors upon

the whaler's coast   Voices torn,
pieced, re-sewn   In lion light,
in whale song, in sleep that follows
lullaby, in wakening of lyric night

song stages history's long speech
reads whaler's voyage, lion's maw
Opens field of ancient voice
Folds its origami: Form

Past

Untrod

cento after Tacita Dean

The riddle of untrodden land
        has risen out of the ocean
        as dawn has risen to the upper ether

The riddle: loading sand
        onto a delirium
        tarnished like dirty metal

And untrodden land: an artefact
        left to rot

—

Modern white
windmills produce
prehistoric
weather and the
speeding
up of time
the sound
the wild
sound of sea
and shingle
beaches, of
a motorbike
passing

at dusk this is
the fake voyage off
the polder

—

This is a fiction. A fiction of sound, a fiction of votive meaning, a fiction all about swollen feet stamped with doubt.

Sleep and death meet off the Isles. Sleep and death—not even rare, places of disrepair, where no man ever trod—produce a salty taste. Heal all ailments.

Haw Count

erasure after S.P.B. Mais

Have you ever played a hillsman away from bleak,
        brooding freedom?
I think we are absences, lost in the climb to meet reality,

                                                            groundless.

        Sky of palest Yorkshire, clogs
        on the cobbles
        a black irregular scar
        —paleolithic monster—
        twilight.

        On one side, a winding
                                shining
                            street
                        —gate—foursquare house.

Descend from the rectory.

Flat tombstones flickering and clogs on the causeways
                                on titanic crags.

——

The open moor:
some dismantled machinery in uncertain light.
Heather and bracken and bilberry and slag-heaps

like polished granite.

Screes look up and across all the world.

The wildest was
, as usual ,
right:

the hill recalls masked faces, faëry ballad.

It ain't a-goin' to rain no mo'!
I'm goin' to coom sweep out

—

Cross to the main door. Fumble out an eerie '*Sst! Sst!*'

(Why find t'oother door?)

Pass through the eaves, the window-panes,
the black stone walls and shining tombstones.
The tarns and reservoirs. The hillside too.

(Loose stone walls pen
the moor itself. Ruin,

like a bent witch walking
into cotton-grass.)

Hilltops stand under the beam of keen clear light.

Wildness   a muddy brown beck in a narrow ravine
a hamlet of moors
its real name stubbed with nails
like the packhorse bridge

The whole moor wrapped in forbidding day.
The strange crabbed writing
where haunting has least rubbed off;
is scarcely striking.

The Queen's Ocean

Aqua—aquamarine—sea green—
colour names she heard applied
to the waters she had never seen,

would never see. The world was stripped
from her upon stepping into France, then
recreated in her hands. A garden and

its still canals curled through her own *hameau.*
Opulent, then simple, then become
the Widow Capet, in strange enclosure

her imagination roved beyond
the cell, beyond the *Conciergerie*, tiptoed
slipshod up to the waves

she could not quite picture—at Calais,
at Le Havre, at Brest, at Point-de-Grave—
and finally beyond. She never saw the ocean.

Remember the day the news arrived at Court?
Cook, the voyager, gone. The sudden tears
her appropriate brine, shed for hours

spent pondering the globe a mere queen
could not traverse. Grief
lagged, nipped at his far-off corpse

a full year later, when the report came through,
and lingered later still as she pulled the volume
of his explorations closer in her tower.

Now known only by number,
Prisoner 250 let the familiar words once more
swim before her eyes—

In the PM
hoisted out the Pinnace
and Yawl in order

to attempt a landing
but the Pinnace
took in water so fast…

All that water! So much that,
unlike that pooling at Versaille,
at last it appeared to be *sea green*.

All that water.
Another world, an Oceania. All
that water, and her fate, risen above the tower.

At Skagen

Suddenly I understand why each
body
of water was ascribed its own local god

by the ancients. Waves engage
a battle
that neither body could ever win, knit

into chevron after chevron. Their
contest
heartbeat—the always-sharp meeting

point of water tumbles land
into shape.
And later, four miles away, amid dunes

I watch: wind's wavering
hand
carves and re-carves the day.

Verisimilitude

A film director buys rats.

He buys 10,000 rats. He buys them to release in a pristine, old-world town. He buys them to recreate a moment past, except of course this time the camera will capture it all. He will film the 10,000 rats pulsing through the streets, acrobatically leap-frogging each other to find a way beyond the main drag. All other streets are blocked.

When the rats arrive their colour is inauthentic. Lab-coat white. Impossible to record a plague of 10,000 *white* rats. With vats and cages and a vast bank of hairdryers (lest he lose his investment to pneumonia) the director transforms them. Now grey, they can race backward through the centuries. Now grey, it will be *like real*.

Lighthouse, Cape Otway

A sandstone cone stacked
    on limestone cliff, here
the gash made by human
    loss sealed
with scar of lighthouse:
    until 1994

its Fresnel lens sliced
    the waters uninterrupted
by the tending of successive keepers;
    spliced a safe path
through the shipwreck coast,
    a line through

slur of water, jag of rock
    and stitched each new rudder
to its beacon
    now obsolete,
replaced by the solar light
    that wakens the night

with its three short white flashes
    soaring over waves
every eighteen seconds.

—

A kilometre from the clifftop
        cone, a forgotten place:
the lighthouse keepers' graveyard,
        half-covered with shifting
sand, cooled by fern and blown
        with seed-heads

of dandelions. Here
        the lightmens' families
lie miles from any other
        place, and one stone reads
'Sacred to the memory
        of…' The remembered name

now sunk beneath weed
        and ground. The childrens'
black wrought-iron fences
        resemble cribs in mourning—
and in this dusk I see
        the keeper's hand retrieves

the signal from the light
        so as never again to become
undertaker.

On Bury Art

erasure after S.P.B. Mais

You know Camelot
know that the only true Camelot is a green knoll of midsummer

But you needn't thread every moment with a clock
of Arimathea
with the sacred cup under the Tor
buried between architecture and archaeology.

Be shepherded into fact and fancy. Harbour both—

—

In the Pilgrim's Inn, a loft room is haunted by the panoply of
green rapidity
a palimpsest set on a green hill

white-washed, white
-limed, white smocks and
smocks not so white.

Then another change:

the flat brown road, hedgeless at flood level.

Withies upright at the junction.

—

To reach   the orchards: pull against the door-post
                of the Great Flood
            the monument: flatten between the obelisk
                and the bridge over the Tone
            the withy-bed: sell the unstable canoe, half-full
                of water.

After landing be content with the remnants of a blue silk flag.

(The monument is a severity   of pardon and vigilance, a
                               black piled heap of black
                               shawls, blotted out by grey
                               rain, orientated by the Dog
                               Star. A cinema. A strange
                               obliquity of grandeur.)

And you unravel the tangled skein of rock.
More. Of grail.

Utopia / After Oz

The storm blows you back
        its funnel ardent
        its wide hungry eye
Its tongue croons you
onto flatline of prairie

When poppies drowsed you
red breath drew
gravity into your limbs:
you yearned for tall grass
a narrow tunnel
of consciousness, brain
heart sharp, nerve

Migrant loess skims west
You root back into plain
        —Call this *home*
        —Call this *no place*
Ground glows like ruby
dense and knotted
as blood

Study of a lion

In black chalk the beast
brusques forward   Silence   Rubens
has stopped his mouth
with a single line   He is already
awed by the den
he will find himself in   even now
as his mane curls into wisp
of emptiness   A study on paper

But there in white chalk the grim
pose brightens
into recognition smudged nose
bent toward the scent
of viewer   Eyes steadily lighting
toward the years one swift textured paw
lifted ever so slightly
Patient as an avalanche

Peat Lea

erasure after S.P.B. Mais

Think of home. The home of your ancestors. Of sun
and a child's alphabet. A Lilliput of words and meadows.
        Blast it with dynamite.

Quarry the veneer of candour, misleading not in size
but symmetry. Say 'starving'. Mean 'cold'. Our ancestors
                        —blue, vast—have been lost.

But underfoot the telegraph wires can be revived
if they keep to the open moor.

——

And limestone country (a philologist; a bibliophile) pumps
day and night throughout the house, church, orchard.
                        Transports ore of honeycomb

in a prehistoric barrow.

        (—In 1665 a box of cloth arrived.
        From that box, the plague.
        Spirits cross under an ancient yew.
        The graves all one calamity.
        Heroism gone down this mine—)

Put on a cap. Bend down. Descend
through solid, wet rock; distant light. A black hole above.
An odd smell everywhere. *Surface*.

(—This business of separation is
a lantern guaranteed not to fail.)

Watching Science Fiction

Before memory takes the graft, the stasis of the past

the *real* past—if there is real anymore—plays like the engine

of a fear whose source is lost, limb and confusion ripped

from the brink of laundered cotton shirts.

—When the memory

takes she does not know it, trigger finger quicker in eidetic

erasure, safe haven remapped but the fit of uneasy synthetic,

the fit of swagger unnatural to body's contour, her face

so familiar. Familiar and lost. The faces around her so normal,

watchful and careful flooded. Flooded with false harmony.

Gynandromorph

Born *both*, the butterfly
wears the jewel of *she*
and the soot-like shroud of *he*:

the brilliant eye of red
not met with symmetry
on the creature's other blackened

wing. Mismatched, chimerical
she traces the quiet breeze
he beats the air staccato

and, one mind,
it alights on twig or leaf
sucks nectar in the heat.

Jonah

The '*greate fyshe*', terrible
colossus, dark cathedral of days
and nights, arrests
lost Jonah in his flight. Three

days and nights spent
in wet earnest prayer, dread
dowse of whale's
appetite, drowse of oceanic

will. It is a liturgy
of krill. A pinwheel spun
in blur of hope, despair.
The shroud of stomach's wall,

grave chamber, draped
in sacred bile. Three days lost.
Three nights. Till their
cadence, *amen*, resolves.

Aged

Here he is in the web magazine. His shell swelled to full size more than a hundred years past, a roving hillock on an island almost no one remembers.

Come from the other side of Africa, ashore. Evidence over a century old: bearing the sepia tint of the Boer war. Colonial soldiers standing formal for a portrait with the patriarch. And now a journalist from the national broadcaster come to pay respect on her knees. She greets the blind old lump with fruit. His neck expressive, skin sagging with authority.

He has earned a probable superlative: he is, most likely, ______*-est*. And so it is already planned. Protocols codified, site pre-consecrated, obit already on file in the newspaper office. Some kind of emperor, his subjects may not live to see his last sea-fall. But they have been its architects. The future will execute their vision.

Daybreak

The dawn is only a thought.

The fulcrum on which we rest our newsprint,
our toothless fingerprints, our balmy Paxil days.

Only a thought of the windy, dwindling kind.

Wake to urgent messages, to the waltz of hours crisp
and fragile as thin pastry. To roulette of lightning yes.
Of arid no.

Borderland

cento after Siri Hustvedt

In that borderland between the icon and the human face
there is a map of the landscape, the ruins, the city, the sky,
the lightning—

a map more durable than other kinds of memory.

That borderland between the icon and the human face:
a stream runs between them, covered by thick glass.
The ground augurs

reverie with the blurriness of an out-of-focus snapshot

and the stream augurs a future bridge. In that borderland
between icon and human face, feathered and naked
birds wear

the heads of men. There's a monkey. There's a monocle.

Now ankles revert to hooves. Again, we see shoe soles.
The weather is bad, but nobody seems to notice.
And a man in a fur coat looks

like an owlish black cat, himself his own figment.

Watching Science Fiction

The one wanders in the woods searching for a beacon while

the other succumbs to quantum events entanglement to

memory. A different self a taloned gulf between self and self

between self and votive lover paved over by the letting go.

The question

asks itself. *Who am I?* We perfume ourselves with a hint of rot

in order to bear unbearable sweetness. We overwrite this life

with life unlead with *what if* with our stumbles. We recall

perfectly the unlived version. We just accept like plumed

Novalis that *memory is what is present*. Now who are we? Now

the other asks in these streetcar woods who are we?

Separation

How else to proceed
but to wear
this loneliness
as precious necklace?

See: clasp rusted
into closure, jewels
stricken on my collarbone,
brittling like hunger.

I could wear sadness like rags,
myself become frayed
into nothingness, but don't—

Listen. The baubles clang together
—Like music.
—Like more noise.

Or / All

erasure after S.P.B. Mais

I came to the early saints over hillsides.

    Limit desire   Sit still
    during incidents of life

Commemorate it. Reread the riotous colour of grace.

I climbed once—900 feet above sea level.

    Hear the tormented ghost
    A limpet-shell chased by Eternity

I know black peat, whistling on the horizon, to be bottomless.

    Return to singing   Defy midnight
    Listen   or look   A solitary curlew
    and a solitary snipe in full bloom
    their way the safest   Also the best

(Follow them all the way down; refuse maps.)

    Without compasses   without watches
    day could scramble about on kistvaens
    A sob or a gasp of peridot or dusk

And I scarred the wind and the tamarisks and a chough.

> Gathering the edge of the island in its
> chimney-pot   This sea walk jingles

Walked in a trance through combes, zigzagging
like an elephant's trunk.

> Like paradise   Like the tide-line empty
> of ships   Waiting for two brothers   One
> weak   The other wizened   Both drown

The last wolf was killed. A carrion-crow muffled the island
with time. A funicular travelled an inch into slate.
Grey. Green.

> I said   I left unsaid   Colours split want

Assay

Darling, against the night
stand hours
of day

[Dickinson, 135: *Water—is taught by thirst*]

: be conscious. That is all
I learned, standing at the northern tip
of empire.

[*Land—by the Oceans passed*]

Your words arrive on air.
I have missed you. Past tense, perfective—
reality shaped by what is now true. I / you.

Our dirt
inscribed with hope
worked through with aspiration.

Wolf

His garish hunger was prayer
His naked leap for the throat more ardent prayer still
His teeth jewels precious and painful as gift of cut diamond

And revenge merely human
Split apart by amateur surgeon patched together rough
Hands lacking antiseptic finesse

What hunger could remain?
Innards fine-tuned and filtered through weight of guilt
Until the stones in his belly were nothing but grief

Empire

Five winters
stone has kept my fingers
agile

Reaching into coat's
warm pocket
hand navigates ancient Plovdiv

in a piece
of gravel—weather's shrapnel—
as my old

coat's wool weaves heat
into my skin
All this

stone's patient indifference
observes in
press

of passing seasons
All this discarded time
reflected

in petroglyph's striation
as now
the oil of human

hands laid on
as now their second
hand

fever warms
a fragment of lost Thrace
lost empire

Pequod

cento after Dan Beachy-Quick

Charged electrically but darkly:
the whale by the whale's own light
swallows illumination, finds again
        the finite pull of song

The body bears the text
of distances covered
of uncharted regions of the globe
        —Pursuit is *what he knows*

And light exasperates the world
—a terrible storm and terrible calm—
until the keystone sun
        nails the coin to the mast

Ash and Rough

erasure after S.P.B. Mais

A tour through instinct
needs a day of smoothest
virtue. (It is very little visited.)

e.g.] Wednesday morning the wind portended
sadness, and the morning paper
described sleep, white bull in repose.

My object was to copy the wildness of snow
climb the steepest way up into a deposit
of soft light, eventually piercing the loose
black shale of words. My consciousness:
the postman delivering a blizzard.

(Withstand the strange
pot-holes descending into
subterranean antiquity,
its stirrup.)

Q.] *Whose memorials are to be seen in the horse-shoe,*
in the Ordnance Map?

A.] *The walkers walking where no one else walks.*
In outlawry. In shriek of austerity.

Chimera

Cupped by dirt then buried   learning in earth blindness to
feel history passing   the chimera reads the tracery of the city
erupting overhead as Arezzo inhales, sighs

Hands reach into trenches   dug to lay the city's new walls   and
grapple a monster's body of bronze   into air, his
three treacherous faces alert

The fortress looms, and the piazza   thick with human fears
Chimera watches as stones are laid   into new streets

Awakening to brilliance   and overwhelmed with light
he witnesses some new faith arising   on the floodplain

Claws splay   at the boundlessness of air

Knothole

cento after Hans Zinsser

The themes of the minister's eulogy travel
on the wings of the tsetse fly. They stalk us
in the bodies of rats—waylay us
in spoilt air—(the air spoilt by mice).
There is a heavy feeling in the limbs. Fear
of eulogy's administrative logic.

The minister's eulogy is a temple
already looted by soldiers, the minister himself
the keeper of a leprosarium founded in the root
tubercles of clover, in rotting wood and refuse.
The eulogy, the leprosarium, just knotholes
into the minor details of intimate life.

Eradication, South Georgia

O Brown Rat! Common Rat! Sewer
and Wharf Rat, *Rattus*
norvegicus!
        your success at roving, settling, fails
only at the southmost hurdle

and now your human competitors,
the other settlers, throw aloft a confetti
of poison pellets—

they quiet your chirps
and your bruxing
        with the balm of eradication.

Yes, the fat Pintail chicks
have been rescinded
from your paycheck,

        the tundra dwellers
do not want you—Waterfront Blemish,
Ice Cove Minx—

so do not don your hairshirts,
do no penance for daring
to follow your whalers…

You can steer clear
of the try pots, burrow with your pack,

but the bluff will lure you,
toxic hailstones rain down upon you.

Nor Borrow

erasure after S.P.B. Mais

In cathedral cities, factory chimneys.

A gabled inn bearing the inscription
Common Lands
is full.

Flemish weavers pass blue and green respects
to the verger.

In his study, the Abbot gushes along the winding maze of the church.

(I could hear a much
freer and lovelier
heart striking the end
of day.)

A beacon plays odd pranks in the marshes.

Shallow water edges over the landscape.

Trawlers populate the tiny attic of a Spanish admiral.

(I saw the actual scalp
of Agincourt.)

(I saw the grave of
the silk mercer's son:
a small plot of grass
carved out of May.)

Prayer for Any Morning

If I believe in prayer it's all a prayer—
tatty hours (cherish / the broken) made up
of praise and plea

A drill chitters outside the window
Stutter out of sleep's wax, sleep's
gauzy orison

into a holy reverie
breakfast and wakeful loneliness—
for what is loneliness but

awareness I am human? (/ cherish
the broken) What is that awareness
but an act of praise?

And in the seamless ordinary
bills unpaid, plants unwatered, library
books still unreturned, a sweater yet

half unknit, and unslippered feet
(cherish the / broken) They curl with the chill
in which they woke

Say it / again—

cherish the broken
monuments / days

Elegance

cento for Luke Carman

A thorn in your throat beats a leathery rhythm:
        West, endless west—

Sun like a blood clot. Mud just beneath
the grass of unassuming front yards.
All those yards like something glanced

in the rear view mirror. And old buildings
just take up space. Yawning windows face the concrete
blocks of a new carpark. Barred shopfronts flicker
        phantasmic blue.

I guess you're like a minor Aussie character
in movies, knife concealed in your shoe,
loud in your little apartment.
The ordinary answers orbit like atonal sadness

And you always keep chance in your coat pocket
        —so you write cover letters to nowhere.
You always remember you can fall and fall again.

Charm to Cover New Ground

Mark the starting place
        trace in stone the origin
of want's propulsion—

cairn-step. Leaf tattle.
        Startle undergrowth, ground,
with ire's expulsion.

Walk straight, walk bent (no matter)
        enter quick thicket
of mind's dwelling.

Stone-borne, clay-borne.
        tell all progress to Echo.
Record Echo's retelling.

Watching Science Fiction

Stood at a grave the whole story up till now unravelled—

our son not *our* son our son instead something necessitating

the word *instead*. A father's grief retrieved him from a different

world that grief a ferryman poling between worlds. What coin

pays the fare besides the one with the non-president's head

the history that also comes instead?

The son not even aware

of his loneliness the loneliness a landfill filled in with the

hand-me-down memories that come from before come from

the *first one*. Instead he recalls each time remembering

nothing of childhood nothing except his father gone worldless

gone mad with guilt traversed vibration's rattling grief.

Decline and Fall

cento after Eliot Weinberger

Retreated to a barren island—

Retreated through their narrow tunnels—

Retreated into mouse-holes and crevices—

(Forgotten kingdoms lie there in the mud
Where the only food is dirt
Where 'dirt' stands in for 'wrath')

Present

Day Trip on a Visit Home

In the two years since I'd seen her last
she'd gotten married—
they'd even, she told me, tried for kids

and settled into suburban bliss, half dreaming
of new lives.
With embarrassment, or guilt, or both,

she told me of her honeymoon in Thailand,
that week of tourist-
brochure pleasure, chosen over

a trek through small towns in middle America,
looking up distant friends.
She told me all this as we drove

along Highway #1 together. Then across
a laminex table
as we sat in a café two hours out of Melbourne

she confessed 'I don't know why we're friends,'
as though she felt the life
she'd chosen was too small, as though

the hours and days they spent driving across the Nullabor,
just the two of them,
were not a vast enough vision of the world—

as though my own succession of modest, rented rooms
in differently-accented cities
was not also a reduction of a keen ambition.

As though the intimacy of our ten years
of shared conversation
were just a prelude to the words voiced

at last—*too* little, *too* distant, *too*——. Until
I reached out
and touched her hand, reminding her

of the long roads we'd driven before, journeys made
to see a stretch of water,
or a monolithic rock I'd come across

in some book and hatched a plan to see. I reminded her of
her willingness each time
to be astonished giving me permission

to plan the next excursion. Slipping once again
into the car
we followed the curved road

those last ten minutes to the lookout,
and saw the vast
volcanic plain, a world rolled out

beyond mere sight, and looked to either side—
                    east and west we saw the shrunken lakes,
          the ones that usually bore the description

'largest,' contracted beneath the cloudless sky.

Future

Dispatches from Earth

cento after Sir John Mandeville

I

I shall tell of all the towns and cities
I shall tell of all the castles
I shall tell of the hand, a round apple of gold

        I, John Mandeville, saw this well

Some embark at the city of Geen
Some want to travel to Tartary
and others live under the planet called Saturn

Say that the ox is the holiest animal
Say that on earth rats may be as big as dogs
Say there is neither correct faith, nor a perfect law

        I, John Mandeville, saw this well

II

Let's load the ships with salt
        instead of balm

Let's load the ships with calamus
        and not the oil of mercy

The cedar does not rot
        The hawthorn has many virtues

and hemlock and nettles flow out
        of the Terrestrial Paradise—

III

Each city is a hill
of salt and
heaven
falls on the
herbage

Paradise is
a loch
—and it
has
no bottom

Charm for Heart's Protection

Take to bed a rodent's whisker
        Remember: artful love's a trickster

love's a clown—
        eat its sweetness, wash it down

Take to bed the jaded moon
        and breathe into its little lung

then exhale the empty scent
        of crater's darkness, lava spent

Take to bed a river stone
        dream yourself a salmon—roam

counter-current, flick and leap
        free and hard ahead in sleep

Arch, ebb, order

erasure after S.P.B. Mais

'Happiness' is the first word ruined.
'Happiness' is the first word of unrest.

[the white rime
on the vicar-
age magpie-
coloured the will-
o'-the-wisp mist
lemon-yellow
or invisible]

—We eat this quarried stone.

——

Outline the Welsh mountain in the fish lying in glass cases,
a courtesy of perish weight
And the river, white-faced, wearing a black hat of Bridge
cut off from the other side of night
Valley fog—so wide that it looks like the moor itself—
ran down the windows
A medley of bulrushes rose to the grey-shingled roof

——

So whose ghost is happy at last?

The bride of the deep ruts
The Bishop of that grim border
A farmer of Kerry sheep out East,
who sleeps between peaks

——

Filled with yearnings
Turn to the falls a-foaming
Look, my fellow, see.

——

ivy-clad ruins
flow through the woods full
of memories of
the earliest days

so the jackdaw lies

in the print of
green

Where fire had been

Intercontinental

Now sunlight gores the day
invites
autopsy of shadows
makes unlikely myth
of night:

    nocturnals may never emerge
    —on this side

I think of you, bitten
by sharp-mawed
dark

Instances of shining hang
bas-reliefs
mounted on your thick hours

    What traversal?

Words
guddle in the twilight
of intercontinental flight

Words
that needle absence
across the mind

Yet

    we walk a common metre
    weigh a common kilogram

make of day and night (my
day, your night)
an Esperanto

Balcony 2

after Brett Whiteley

I

At play on the harbour the boats glide like fine teacups
turned down, an oh-so-perfect
silver service carted between green
fingers of earth sculpted by water—

water the ultramarine of aggressive
stillness.
                Yes, water has carved
        that homecoming welcome of inlets.

In shadows great palms lean over the scene,
while a bird,
        white,
                kites overhead;

there, too, a tree dusky as late summer plums

        and, distant, a bridge draped like white muslin
in a lazy arc across the blue field.

II

Step back—put hand out to rail. Step back again.

A window frames these catalogued astonishments

Evening. Lights promise that marvellous human shuffle, yonder.

III

Forget the easy postcard gloss: when faced again
        with the real thing the matte of blue and white
bids us look beyond familiar sight:
                the smooth stream of light met *there* and *there*
by snarl of paint. The simplest tools engulf:
here sweep of vertical line—here met by horizontal flight.

        So that's the *fidget with infinity*...

Look—and somehow see. We too are at first waterborne;
        then, at last, borne on air.

Berg

A fin of ice   arising out of sky, frigid sea   A single turret
above belies   the monolith beneath   The berg advances
at the speed of a pilgrim   travelling   on foot

Calved from huger sheets   and carved, desolate   its drapery,
its skirts   submerged

The berg   at a palmer's pace   dissects the waters

And you: First anatomise the cryosphere   Breathe

out   ever-condensing vowels   Capture its face   then explode
the berg   bring the wreckage   to light

Affair

cento after W. G. Sebald

No one at the ticket desk.
No one at the lock-keeper's cottage.

  He moves like his own ghost
  on a brittle strip of celluloid:
  nothing visible but the sky.

Events cut like a film

—the silver bracelet, the ageing skin,
the jumble of curios arranged
on the shelves (plates,
porcelain cups, plaster busts…), an extra
in evening dress, the rubble
in time—

decked out with a love story.

  Ghosts do not vanish until cockcrow.
  Ghosts do penance in the dark.

Laboratory

Little monks clothed in white
they take their petty tasks
in stride, no mind for risk just
turn the slender wheel
of their mortality

—Little monks. Set a-quiver
in communal prayer of fever
injected with some human
cancer, soon perfected
into specimen.

Little hearts: their atria
hold wonders. Little lungs
expand, exhale. Little
cells—peal of matins, vespers.
Knell of self. Of selflessness.

Record

cento after Ali Smith

This is the story of my tattoo. Look
at my lip. Look at my hip bone.
Like an ancient baked tablet. Like
the face of a clock—but a clock
with a thin layer of dust
on its face. A clock with the heart
of an apple tree. This is
the story of my tattoo. Look at
my hip bone. Crystalline
like the egg of a bird. Hollow
and full. Stately and weighty
through to the platelet level.
My hip bone. Like the bare trunks
of the trees. Shines green.
A jolly engraving of the old
Roman road in the wood. So much
for my Artful Dodger pockets.
This is the story of my tattoo.
It hurts like irony.

Watching Science Fiction

Reminds us of a story. The one about cheap hotels changed identities brief encounters. The one that offers no solace. Reminds us of a story that leaves him hiding in the shabby wardrobe singing *Row Row Row* in gravelled madness. Reminds us that he always arrives somehow asks the simplest question

The rest of it the cellular mitosis

the tramp through all those tawdry off-road places a last image imprinted on the retina the recaptured body electric... We imagine ourselves into that place of horror. Reminds us when he asks avuncular *were you safe* of that voice in the exhausted corner singing...*Life*...*dream*...

Or: Fell / Dale

erasure after S.P.B. Mais

Taken over the unknown
        hills to these grass
                fells we crossed and
                        recrossed

the broadest dales—a raid
        on the roofless
                memory of a woman

in this manner wooed
in this manner won

her sadness

—not associated with memory (it
                doesn't stand on rock; its
                        vaulted room like
                                a hedgeless road)

—a lovely mountain. Her strata
                flow through the heart:
                        ideal gills and becks
                                down the fell-

side of the smooth summit. Suddenly,
changes, ruins.
The great keep

Here I
Here is

reflected in the

one-o'clock-to-three quake

are wild and fair
are green

of the thunderous dark.
A lady is
a toll-bridge

dignified by her cup of milk.
Muttering

Let those
Lest those

turning away

shed thy light
spoil to-night

pull the curtain aside and

thy blaze, O
the feet of

rush

to the white waste
        of strange black a road
                to the wound, to
                        the trace

of the lover—the afternoon
    a double S
        zigzag across
            and across the hills.

Simulation

Scientists run simulated voyages into space.

Whenever real rockets take off, a shadow crew sequesters itself in a warehouse. In tandem with updates sent from *out there* the astronauts complete the mundane tasks of passage. Safety check. Safety check. Safety check.

When an emergency message comes through, the crew throw themselves against walls in empathy, snap their necks left and right with force and actual terror. When the reports are confirmed—the shuttle has burned up—they play dead. Hours later, they are still afraid to let anyone know they are awake. All this time, one has been tapping Morse code into the palm of his crewmate. Every minute or so a silent wail: I-A-M-B-U-R-N-I-N-G.

Watching Science Fiction

The bodies turned gelatinous the bodies as if in aspic and

the feds called in is it disease or is this assault. Liaison's glance

a razor drawn across the airplane's aisle across the hospital

corridor across the oceans till the son throws it back at

gamble's coda. *We all love someone who's dying*.

The gelid body

some deep sea wonder retrieved to air its raucous frailty

under the finger tips its appearance its own X-ray. Liaison

at the keyboard finding answers, finding revelation. Love.

We love. We all love someone. Who's dying.

Conder's Dandenongs

after Charles Conder

Unpeopled, Condor's long view
to the Dandenongs sings in burned and whitened
tones, the foreground rooted in grasses
and eucalypts. The flats lie open

in the horizontal sweep of rusted ground.
The dizzy view first downward
then beyond the impression of a tea tree,
the path of the river below marks

the city's lonely edge.

The first record of a half-hour's view.
Dust-coloured smoke erupts.
In the background, where the sky meets the blue ridge
something like a spinnaker arises and

sets the horizon to flight.

Wayfaring

cento after Rebecca Solnit

'Lost' is a puzzle-patchwork—brown
        coffee and yellow eggs,
rivers, stores, jails, ferries—
                a map of all the places a criminal

is wanted. Wanted like a lost umbrella,
        lost keys, lost toys and baby
teeth. (Such tokens are possessed
                by their own appetites:

they are saddled with desires like
        experimental films;
like fiddles and the twang of colour.
                Of copper rattles. Coral beads.)

Lost is—and is not—a contagious
        panic. A compass
arguing with the map. Distant blue
                sheep, blue shepherd.

The blank space between saints
        and patrons. It is *us* in blue houses. Where
we piss blue for days. Honey turns to dust.
                We go to hell. —Keep moving.

(Do.) (Try.)

erasure after S.P.B. Mais

Not exactly unknown
but known to be   : no light, no bottom, no breakwater
                                         no parapet

Wonder is neither accident nor red cloak, is
                                a very strange stranger

                dignified and absurd,
                a crown rimmed by shod soldiers full of beauty...

A miracle the only haven in charred gorse
                a rabbit with eyes fantastically in bloom

Two cliffs, orange cliffs, sweep along the altar, and on, on

Earthworks dug up   : the heart under the ancient yew
                                     the skull leading down the wooded walk
a shallow blush from a restless world, brooding
                                                    in sympathy with winter

Nobody knows
                                beyond human conjecture

deepest blue a lofty room

furtive love

a risk worth taking

After 'The Fisherman and His Wife'

Walk to the water. Un-dam your desires.
Fall into a *pas-de-deux* with the tide.
And when the flounder comes,
both eyes sunny-side up on his flank,
throw him back
throw him deep—
the ocean floor is his true north.

Throw him with ardour, and
whisper your every caprice.

    The shack turned to a cottage,
    cottage to palace, palace to papal seal—
    all that flashes in his weird eyes.

Only the ever-changing calligraphy
of waves sweeping the shore
records the moment. Then it's gone.

Walk to the water, and ask too much.
    It is all that can be asked.

Still Life

cento after Siri Hustvedt

I know where yonder is.

Yonder is how the brain works in the borderland of dream

and memory

in the empty space of light between maps

of possible pleasure. Between scuffles of desire. Reach out

to take a grape. Take two, alike and interchangeable as two

yonder pears. It's hard to see in the yonder bad light.

In the dim twilight. Real bread goes stale,

real sausage decays. We didn't see the same event.

Words conceal. But as long as we can detect the strings we see.

Yonder: a cork, a boot, a sole, and a bottle.

Future

Passage

Melt has brought about
reunion
Bowheads from both sides

—Pacific, Atlantic—meet in
the middle
press together century-old grazes

from their brushes with
the whalers
(Soon enough we'll find

the jade, the slate, the ivory
sharps
lodged in blubber: we'll retrieve

short-circuited trail-
blazers
that could not ply through

a full half-metre of chub)
They've found
the northwest passage again

the whales, and they idly chase
swimmerets
race into waters once attempted

by *Erebus*, by *Terror*   Yes
they find
themselves where Franklin's men

were lost—where two ships'
worth
of eager nerve were taken out:

starvation; hypothermia; lead
poisoning;
scurvy; dread *consumption*—

for them the passage never
found
What they did find, *could* find

just an endless chill of loss
preserved
for the coming centuries

It's here the bowheads
spyhop
noses up, eyes at waters' level

it's here they exchange
probing
stares, and then stare beyond

—down a lonely newly open
highway
empty but for whales

Did any of them witness
Franklin's
final terror, the grisly hour when

the document was written?
Alongside
the crews' last remnants the simple

lines *Whoever finds*
this paper
...*Quinconque trouvere ce papier*...

Finderen af dette Papiir...Their
testimony
drives the new adventurers

Even now they go in search of
the lost
wrecks, in search of the tatters of some

'heroic' age But *Terror*
is a history
of land; *Erebus* a paean

to a chaos of white nights
on ice
Now Bowheads rise from the sea

drive thick skulls against
the sheet
as they come to find

each other, heads full of
baleen, ice
howl and magnetic pull of *north*

plumb the solitaire deep
keep time
by the minute-hand of floe's

advance and pass each other
in a season's
song, allegro, warming into future tense

New Observance

Quick, the end of worn day

stammering into leaf-bare treetop
crow-sharp, ear
to trunk

sap's glacial ooze
clawing into this thing we call a body

—I recount a ritual descent by ladder

—You, encounter with long oil slick of eel

this elemental radiance
by necessity an instance of terror

Now, in muted room
cusp of night flares onto a screen
as if cued by tilt of

darkling mind

Card and Cast

erasure after S.P.B. Mais

Driven there by rivers I expected
stags and a bright tunnel of green
expected byroads crowned with gypsy
caravans

Indeed, a lonelier cover, sand like slate
sand a blizzard swept up, up
over blinding rain
in an ordinary upland

A stream running through a storm
a border kept alive (gates
all painted red, the soil red, red
as churches) by flood

Through a window a glimpse
white lambs in the byre, lonely
in the kingdom of rats

Four bishops and the word
        'slain'
tomb and brass
canon and rain

The eight mile stretch of sands
The wheels made sand
The long yellow marram-grass an ideal
of sand
Sand drawing a map of mind

Broken stairways and battlements
Cove and Coracle
Two by two

A ruin built on sand, a four-masted wreck
a road-mender on a cart-
horse, a terrace on which foxes used to stand

The mullioned windows
worn away by possession, by
silhouetted sky

Eulogy

after Krystof Kieślowski

Why invent laws if they exist?

Half an hour's wait for luggage
and the law kills the boy.

The boy holds on to 380 volts
then appears four more times

as a ghost. The law is a knife
and a set of compasses. Anyway
he's dead, like most of them.

A strange vacuum forming
around him, the kettle boils

over. There are his damn teeth
in the mud beneath some absurd

two-storeyed tower. Some law.

A Record

cento after Isabelle Eberhardt

One day this notebook of mine
(the notebook
that barks all night long
with its grocery
bills and tailor's invoices)
will end in the total silence of the desert
(the first
thing we do in life
is sleep, transparent on
the white sand)
and at last I will carry in my bundle
(when the notebook no
longer crows like a
rooster, beats
its tambourine)
only a silent ocean's pure white waves

Ennui

cento after Mark Strand

With all that elegiac grace you clear a space for yourself.

It's so big, so empty.

It is the place we shall leave our own bones.

But for now its floor is slippery, and you are blind.

I try to extricate myself. I drink some coffee.

All the hills—like crumbs and place cards
littered on the floor—are actually the same hill.

And we are like hopeless utopians, living for the end.

Nor Angle In

erasure after S.P.B. Mais

When in confidence they risk assertion it is as light-hearted as hot milk. Perhaps the same eyes trace antiquity in the spray of waves, the black trail of smoke. An island rock. A red suspension bridge. *These* lay, saint-haunted, remote—where poetry flourished.

Poetry, a firm sand blowing over reed-covered, black-headed gulls and above water—or is it the world? A fleece, full of oil and yellow light. A soft Arcadia.

And ancient, the strangest hue. A song of precipitous ruin

'records a sigh, a murder or a groan'

Past four o'clock. Their home after death a cathedral bell.

In the hills and slate-quarries they loom. An odd ghost tracks the clouds, lambs in the pasture. Too much wildness bewilders distance, direction. *Pass an age. Think it a day.*

(Without… without… without…)

Mouse

Cut out a sixth of the heart.
At a day old—furless,
close-eyed, resembling nothing
so much as an infant's thumb—
he can survive it.
The mouse can regrow that missing part
in three short weeks.

Aesop knew it:
to be mouse-hearted
is as good as wearing
the swagger of lion.

His heart
perhaps the size of a Lilliputian walnut.
Barely a mouse, already
ripped apart.
He does not wait
for a Godhand to put him back together.
Alone he blindly furrows toward wholeness.

Draft of Days

Once again   talk of loss   *tallest*
of fanged *torquere*   shame
of stasis—   *as is*

I/   erase the border
we   elide the edge in which 'you'
                        break off from 'me'

Shining out in the dimming   *shine dim*
room   their new invention glides
onscreen   a robot jelly-   *e'en hell*
fish   fuelled on hydrogen—   *again*

I/   and only yesterday
we   the robot cheetah's new
                                  landspeed record
                                  for our kind

Mourning Charm

Soot-rigged   bitter earthly
Soot   Psalmist of remains

What façade   What heartburn
What minor song and   minor key?

What spice   What laurel
What Judas tree?

A Monday

cento after Roland Barthes and James Schuyler

The metallic racket of airports
a localised deafness

                                        a flat condition
subject to the edge of a torn look

—experience this as a gust of life.
A radical gesture.

And *Voila*. Home now.
Starting to write a letter
made out of phrases too fine
to be called a skin

and the view shivers with the reticence
of intimacy.

A situation with no offer of lightness.

Line up and face the sun.

Lost

after Frederick McCubbin

A girl alone in the scrubland, her blue
dress melting into bluish leaf
Why the melancholy brought by a single word
or do we know her fate without reading it   *Lost*
The treetops know it   They clear a path to let
the sun beat down on her straw hat
and the grass yellows round her grey stockings
Unruly squawks linger behind the weird silence
unframed   Only the underside of her apron
still white   Only her apron and the terrible sky

Watching Science Fiction

This is grief. The absent son never stands before you but
always at periphery. Never offers CPR just stops the heart
in each reflective surface. So you turn every mirror to the wall
sheathe every silvered face of plate of cup of distorting spoon.
Every convex face is shaped like anguish. Voice splinters
the laboratory and its familiar frequency busts up the silence
fractures your attempts at solace.

When you turn to your
science to explain it nothing pierces the mystery of loss. The
loss was years ago the loss never happened the loss is there at
your side just behind you. Take grief take hauntedness take
the amoral wail of three a.m. Forget the skin. Self is fenceless.
In some unwritten future there's a law of physics to explain it.

Future-Perfect

cento after Eliot Weinberger

You throw ink on a piece of silk
in echo of a grief that is hardly human.

—Grief for that which is already burnt,
like bones collected and preserved in the throat

—Grief: the plant that is always surrounded
by darkness. The past is always in front of you.

A vision of paradise washed of soot everyday.
A vision of paradise never recuperated.

To Peter Rabbit in the Night

for Christopher Eichler

We're outmatched by darkness—
the night unrolls and unrolls
and we *see* them, the rabbits,
hurtling into the charcoal atmosphere,
flashing their incandescent
cottontails behind them. Those tails
a last flashing code from the outskirts
of it all. They're pelting,
open-mouthed, into nothing.
And we're left here, Peter: our heads
poked dreamily out of the warren,
ardent wonderers under the stars.
They say that soon it won't only be rabbits.
—Soon rivers and geese, whales
and hilltops will follow, trailing
the sun and her acolytes until
the cosmos ends our archaeology of light.
And then, Peter, as gravity fails you and me,
our small wonder will briefly mingle
in the emptying sky.

Then Lie

erasure after S.P.B. Mais

The journey north is treeless
                    a world of grass and houses
                                        a pastoral of ascent
                    of black hills, white unknown mountains
and stags, feeding on the snowline
                              on perpetual memory

Retrace the grey crags, the end of everything
Talk about the gash of rock cut
                    by cascades, by a small
                                        upland loch
and reach the haunt of a hut-circle

Repeat the word: 'impossible'

                              as if forever
                              as if you see, north, the border

Fable

cento after Siri Hustvedt

Think of the troubadours. Think of Gatsby.

Think of a small pink man and his pink ox.

> Of hands in a gooseberry bush. An orange lying in the
> refrigerator box. Which has become a home. To think
> like this is to master a dimming past.

Dig and you shall find your own body alive

in its shallow arc, acting the part of a solemn mourner.

> Witness the chattering play-by-play: the ball changes
> hands. Or a note with the words *Je t'aime*. *Je t'aime*:
> the beaded orange heart of an open daisy—

It's not clock time necessarily

when Odysseus finally comes home.

> You can't pay your electric bill. You're stuck. It is bitter
> to hear birds dull and interchangeable as postcards.
> A guillotine hangs over your perfect marble house.

Notes

Untrod: Text is drawn from the extended interviews in *Tacita Dean: The Conversation Series 28* and from the artist's own writings in the monograph *Tacita Dean*.

Haw Count: All text is gleaned from the essay 'Haworth: Brontë Country', from S.P.B. Mais's book *This Unknown Island*.

The Queen's Ocean: I first encountered the story of Marie Antoinette's interest in the 'discovery' of Australia in Antonia Fraser's *Marie Antoinette: The Journey* which I 'read' in audio format. The italicised text is drawn from the *Journals of Captain James Cook*.

Verisimilitude: The story recounted here is inspired by Werner Herzog's account of the filming of *Stroszek* in 1977, as given in Paul Cronin's *Herzog on Herzog*.

On Bury Art: All text is gleaned from the essay 'Glastonbury: King Alfred and King Arthur', from S.P.B. Mais's book *This Unknown Island*.

Study of a Lion: Rubens's 'Lion' (1612–1613) is a chalk study in the collection of the National Gallery in Washington DC, which also displays the painting 'Daniel in the Lions' Den' (1614/1616).

Peat Lea: All text is gleaned from the essay 'The Peak District: Grouse-Moors and Lead Mines', from S.P.B. Mais's book *This Unknown Island*.

Watching Science Fiction: This poem refers to the episode 'Olivia' (Season 3, Episode 1) of the television show *Fringe*.

Gynandromorph: On 12 July 2011 the BBC Nature news reported that a gynandromorph had been born at London's Natural History Museum. A rare half-male, half-female (it is estimated that 0.01% of hatching butterflies are 'sexual chimeras'), this butterfly was especially unusual in that it was perfectly bisected, so that each wing displayed the characteristics of one sex.

Jonah: Referring to the well-known biblical tale, the description 'greate fyshe' comes from William Tyndale's 1534 translation of Jonah 2:1, the literal rendering of the original Hebrew text.

Aged: The subject of this poem is the Seychelles tortoise 'Jonathan', the long-term resident of the island of St Helena, born c. 1832 and believed to be the oldest living land animal.

Daybreak: The italicised text is collaged from Barry Lopez's *Desert Notes & River Notes* and Louise Glück's *Proofs & Theories*.

Borderland: Text is drawn from Siri Hustvedt's essay collection *Mysteries of the Rectangle*.

Watching Science Fiction: This poem refers to the episode 'The Arrival' (Season 1, Episode 4) of the television show *Fringe*.

Or / All: All text is gleaned from the essay 'Cornwall: Bodmin Moor and the Tintagel', from S.P.B. Mais's book *This Unknown Island*.

Pequod: Text is drawn from Dan Beachy-Quick's *A Whaler's Dictionary*.

Ash and Rough: All text is gleaned from the essay 'Lancashire: Pendle and the Trough of Bowland', from S.P.B. Mais's book *This Unknown Island*.

Chimera: This poem refers specifically to the Estruscan bronze sculpture 'Chimera of Arezzo', held in the collection of the Archaeological Museum in Florence, Italy.

Knothole: Text is drawn from Hans Zinsser's *Rats, Lice and History*.

Nor Borrow: All text is gleaned from the essay 'Norfolk: The Borrow Country and the Broads', from S.P.B. Mais's book *This Unknown Island*.

Elegance: Text is drawn from Luke Carman's *An Elegant Young Man*.

Watching Science Fiction: This poem refers to the episode 'There's More than One of Everything' (Season 1, Episode 20) of the television show *Fringe*.

Decline and Fall: Text is drawn from Eliot Weinberger's essay collection *Wildlife*.

Dispatches from Earth: Text is drawn from *The Travels of Sir John Mandeville* in the translation by C. Moseley.

Arch, ebb, order: All text is gleaned from the essay 'The Welsh Arches: The Mary Webb Country and Border Castles', from S.P.B. Mais's book *This Unknown Island*.

Affair: Text is drawn from W.G. Sebald's *Campo Santo*.

Record: Text is drawn from Ali Smith's work *Artful*.

Watching Science Fiction: This poem refers to the episode 'The Same Old Story' (Season 1, Episode 2) of the television show *Fringe*.

Or: Fell / Dale: All text is gleaned from the essay 'The Yorkshire Fells and Dales: Castles, Abbeys, and the "Hand of Glory"', from S.P.B. Mais's book *This Unknown Island*.

Simulation: This poem takes as its inspiration the news reports on the 'Mars 500 Mission' during which six 'astronauts' lived for 520 days in a 'spaceship' housed in the Russian Academy of Sciences' Institute of Biomedical Problems in order to simulate the conditions a crew would undertake on a manned mission to Mars. The mission included a 'Mars walk' and 'return to earth', and 'landed' without incident. The scenario imagined here is a fiction.

Watching Science Fiction: This poem refers to the episode 'Pilot' (Season 1, Episode 1) of the television show *Fringe*.

Wayfaring: Text is drawn from Rebecca Solnit's *A Field Guide to Getting Lost*.

(Do.) (Try.): All text is gleaned from the essay 'Dorset: The Hardy Country', from S.P.B. Mais's book *This Unknown Island*.

Still Life: Text is drawn from Siri Hustvedt's essay collection *Yonder*.

Passage: This poem draws on a story reported on the BBC that, with the advent of ice-melt in the Arctic, the Northwest Passage has opened up in recent summers for the first time in a century, and bowhead whales have been passing through it. Research into bowhead whales indicated that their estimated lifespan is 150 years and that when dying bowheads are discovered, some still have nineteenth-century whaling implements embedded in their bodies. The italicised text is drawn from the letter left behind by the last members of the Franklin expedition before their death: their explanation of their fate was written in seven languages.

Card and Cast: All text is gleaned from the essay 'South Wales: The Cardigan Coast and Pembrokeshire Castles', from S.P.B. Mais's book *This Unknown Island*.

Eulogy: Text is drawn from the work *Kieślowski on Kieślowski*.

A Record: Text is drawn from Isabelle Eberhardt's *The Nomad: The Diaries of Isabelle Eberhardt*.

Ennui: Text is drawn from Mark Strand's essays in *The Weather of Words*.

Nor Angle In: All text is gleaned from the essay 'North Wales: Anglesey and the Mountains', from S.P.B. Mais's book *This Unknown Island*.

Mouse: This poem was inspired by scientific studies reported on the BBC Science news; scientists stated that the research might lead to a greater understanding of the regenerative abilities of the human heart and, more generally, of the newborn body.

Draft of Days: This poem is inspired by the BBC Science news. I have been taking note of the many animalistic robots being produced since I viewed Errol Morris's documentary *Fast, Cheap and Out of Control*, which took as one of its subjects the roboticist Rodney Brooks, former director of the MIT Computer Science and Artificial Intelligence Laboratory.

A Monday: Text is drawn from Roland Barthes's *Mourning Diary* and James Schuyler's *Diaries*.

Watching Science Fiction: This poem refers to the episode 'Olivia' (Season 3, Episode 1) of the television show *Fringe*.

Future Perfect: Text is drawn from Eliot Weinberger's *Oranges & Peanuts for Sale*.

Then Lie: All text is gleaned from the essay 'The Northern Highlands: Prince Charlie's Country', from S.P.B. Mais's book *This Unknown Island*.

Fable: Text is drawn from Siri Hustvedt's *Living, Thinking, Looking*.

Acknowledgements

Poems in this collection have appeared in *ABR, ABR States of Poetry Anthology, The Age, Arc* (Canada), *The Australian, Cordite, Island, The Kenyon Review Online, Meanjin, Rabbit, Eleven Eleven, Red Room Company,* and the anthologies *Best Australian Poems (2009 and 2010)* and *30 Australian Poets*.

Erasures based on the work *This Unknown Island* by S.P.B. Mais appeared in the chapbook *No Land* published by Work and Tumble.

Some of these poems were produced during the year I occupied the role of Sydney City Poet. Great thanks to Arts NSW and University of Technology Sydney for this initiative.

Many people have offered support in the making of this work. I would like to thank Hazel Smith, Linda Gregerson, Kate Fagan, Chris Andrews, Laura Kasischke and Khaled Mattawa for their mentorship over many years. Fiona Wright, Emily Stewart, Nick Tapper and Ivor Indyk for shepherding this book into print. R.D. Wood for championing my erasure poems. Lindsay Tuggle, Claire Nashar, Lisa Gorton, Liz Allen and Toby Fitch for advice and friendship. Zacha Rosen, as well as Alan, Viv and Anahi for their love and support. My parents, Kay and Graham Middleton, for everything.

The Giramondo Publishing Company acknowledges the support of Western Sydney University in the implementation of its book publishing program.

This project has been assisted by the Commonwealth Government through the Australia Council, its arts funding and advisory body.